WHITE CAMPION

WHITE CAMPION

Poems by Donald Revell

Alice James Books
Farmington, Maine
www.alicejamesbooks.org

© 2021 by Donald Revell
All rights reserved
Printed in the United States

10 9 8 7 6 5 4 3 2 1

Alice James Books are published by Alice James Poetry Cooperative, Inc., an affiliate of the University of Maine at Farmington.

Alice James Books
114 Prescott Street
Farmington, ME 04938
www.alicejamesbooks.org

Library of Congress Cataloging-in-Publication Data

Names: Revell, Donald, 1954- author.
Title: White Campion / Donald Revell.
Description: Farmington, ME : Alice James Books, [2021]
Identifiers: LCCN 2020045540 (print) | LCCN 2020045541 (ebook) | ISBN 9781948579179 (trade paperback) | ISBN 9781948579414 (epub)
Subjects: LCGFT: Poetry.
Classification: LCC PS3568.E793 W48 2021 (print) | LCC PS3568.E793 (ebook) | DDC 811/.54--dc23
LC record available at https://lccn.loc.gov/2020045540
LC ebook record available at https://lccn.loc.gov/2020045541

Alice James Books gratefully acknowledges support from individual donors, private foundations, the University of Maine at Farmington, the National Endowment for the Arts, the Amazon Literary Partnership, and the Maine Arts Commission, an independent state agency supported by the National Endowment for the Arts.

Cover art: "Two Plant Specimens" by William Henry Fox Talbot. Credit: Edward E. Ayer Endowment in memory of Charles L. Hutchinson

CONTENTS

I.

Aphasia	1
A Hint to Plotinus	2
Catafalque	4
Senesco sed amo	5
Ingenium nobis ipsa puella facit	8
Deus nec laedit amantes	10
Ubi amor, ibi oculus est	11
Omnia quae sunt, lumina sunt	12
Hate Speech	15
In Memory of Denise Levertov	16
A Hint to Lucretius	17

II.

Easter 2018	21
The Silver Hyphens	23
"The sensation of death . . ."	25
American Sunlight	26
Saved for Later	34
A Doe on a Peach	37
White Campion	38
When I Die	44
The Measure	47
Notes	51

ACKNOWLEDGMENTS

I wish to thank the editors of the following journals in which many of these poems first appeared.

Asheville Poetry Review
The American Poetry Review
Catamaran
Conjunctions
The Harvard Advocate
The Literary Review (TLR)
The Meadow
Plume
Plume Poetry 7
Poetry
Seneca Review

For Kathryn & Geoffrey

*Time reigns; yet the kingdom of love is every moment,
Whose citizens do not age in each other's eyes.*
—Vernon Watkins

I

APHASIA

Herr!...Herr!...Herr! The Saint John Passion
Opens, triumphantly, gates rampant and gates
Weathered green by early love. In no other
Animal but the steed of human music
Does allusiveness bite down on the bridle,
Breaking memory into splinters and shards,
Sowing the bits at speed to become forests,
Arias, and the folly of dead poets.
I must remember as quickly as I can.
On the far side of darkening waters
Frost blooms and thistles forecast thunder.

A HINT TO PLOTINUS

It is because things are the way they are that they are good.

She suffers the least gesture of the oldest tree,
Its latest infant. Too, she is breath to me,
And like the saints whom we've refused,
She comprehends the inward of breath:
A world of shining grass and free animals.

You've seen her. The underside of a leaf
Catching the light of your birthday in—
What was it? A gust of wind? A grimace
Of your angel?—featured exactly
As she was: soft vertex of gray on green.

The wrist of the afterlife curls around
A stem. Immortality comes first
If ever it comes afterwards. Suffer
The rebuke and move on, which is to say
Upwards into the sainted, oldest tree.

At great heights, oblivion
Mimics creation. Disguised as clouds
And flecks of wingspan as once Constable
Hurried them onto the face of clouds,
Preexistence covers the whole earth,
Pillared by trees. Little bubble of breath,
Little hazelnut of lungs, I nearly fail

To feel the sharp reproach in you, so dearly
Do I love the infant of reproach.
Her delay, her light foot at the edge of life

Is shelter to me, all animals
Climbing into the architecture
Even time must recognize as Time itself.
The saints are in hysterics. Oblivion
Mimics creation, and we are free to begin.

CATAFALQUE

In memory of John Ashbery

Angel of the gap thrills to floodwaters
Like a man slapped by a man slapped,
Newsworthy Africa.

How much of the world fits or is navigable
Depends entirely upon the thrilling angels.
Pins and needles, the neural system of
Lacustrine, riverine, and lately
This pain in my groin rising
Creaturely.

Horizon shuns the morning star this morning.
English overtops the trees with prophecy.
Clement waters, misplaced by mountains,
Seek new outlets, finding only
You and me. And I'm not there.

SENESCO SED AMO

Starlight is almost flesh.—Basil Bunting

One life, not one among
A thousand others of quail
Like tipsy mandarins crowding
The cold of a low wall
Along a line of trees, the angel
Promised me and nothing
More, nothing to weigh.

Menippus and Lucian
Be with me now as I
Feel my way among
Misted pillars and ghosts
Of breath on upper Broadway.
A quick kiss in the crosswalk is
More to me than mankind.

There is no middle ground.
There is our empty bench.
There is the stoop of pigeons.
Either I have been alone
Every hour of my life or
Never once, not even
One moment, and the mist rising.

Angel, how stern you have become.
Stricken, almost as strange as Uruguay
Against traffic in the middle distance,
You stride, and there is bread in your step
And sunlight ground into fine powder.
All the same, I feel comforted.
The sharper the mist, the sweeter the hour.

For good reason, enormous windows
Gape the walls of our museums.
Brâncuşi's woman asleep awakes to see
Riotous sunlight feeding the air
Because air is what becomes of light
When no one is looking. Only myself,
And I have never been alone until now.

The stern angel gives me bread and the courage
Of satire. Crossing the street towards me,
Menippus and Lucian extend their arms,
And birds alight upon their arms, shitting,
Cooing. What is mankind to me
When I have remembered a kiss in the night sweats
Against the traffic, without a breath of air?

The word "steadfast" comes to mind, a word
Like "dusk", awaiting its formal elegy
In abandoned train yards. Little fires
In bins are all that remains of English.
I step into the crook of the wing of my
Steadfast angel. I catch the scent
Of newly washed hair, and she says to me

"Shelter here." Satire is shelter *in extremis*.
Christ has the dispatch of it, having
Inscribed bitter verses upon human eyes
For angels' delight and the increase
Of crooked human sleep. Let mankind sleep
Forever. Christ has suffered enough,
And my angel is clean enough to kiss. We kiss.

INGENIUM NOBIS IPSA PUELLA FACIT

> *I am not at all sure that this is the real world
> but I am looking at it very closely.* —Fleur Adcock

Apples whisper into the canvas, a still
Undertone, exactly the mew of an old woman's
Pain at the very end of pain.

Stop shouting. The angel of no society
Already knows you, and has awarded
The apple to another. Remain

Seated. In a very little while,
Something beneath the glitter and rind
You have mistaken for yourself

Dies into canvas. Your life begins.
A shout of an altogether different kind
Wakes a little world on your new skin.

What is beauty if not the extreme
Of pathos turned inward upon itself
There to incandesce in agony

Of self-love, anguish indistinguishable
From God's first touch upon Adam
Who loved his life, who loved his life.

Paul Cézanne has filled your mouth with whispers,
Whispers like water. Now try to pronounce
The word "friendship." At best, the sound

You make resembles a slurry, something like "furniture."
All my life, I've famished one idea after another.
Live for beauty or do not live at all.

DEUS NEC LAEDIT AMANTES

My own breath questioned me:
"Is love's bed always snow?"
In my reply, I breathed
Up into my eyes a cold pillow.

Nearer the end of everything,
I am thinking of poor Shelley's terrible
Episode of eyes, of a great
Injured bird staring at a miracle.

We are not God's fools. We are the fools
Of hawks and of the hawks' prey.
Inside my breath, inside yours,
Undistracted hunters delay

For the sheer pleasure of delay,
Knowing in advance the outcome
Of their pleasure. So it is with lovers.
They lie in snow, each to each a white alarm.

UBI AMOR, IBI OCULUS EST

Flumes of the late-night
21st-century Tzigane
In the tall desert wrong
Even after rain. The white
Asphalt gleams. The car radio
Insists upon race anger
Keen as weather and warfare
But with a heaven to get to,
A shock of empty meadow.

The essential of myself is out there
Walking, aimlessly. Meanwhile,
I drive slowly, keeping the spectral
Gypsy flumes fixed in the mirrors.
A scroll of high sound, suddenly,
Like outrage out of nowhere,
Like God in the beginning, from nowhere,
Breaks into the car. I can see
The mirrors blackened and the radio empty.

OMNIA QUAE SUNT, LUMINA SUNT

They are the same angel: slaves grown old
And shipwrecked mariners, equally
Familiar with dark clouds as with doves,
With how the terrible exchange of love
For pathos blinds the animal in us,
Giving away eyes to the fox cub escaping.

A waterfall I know is also that angel.
There comes a time when zeal
Dissipates into a mist of the beautiful
And then into something like fleshly
Diamond—a torrent above and one below,
Briefly angelic, then imago.

The past is stronger than life because it cannot
Be altered. At the precipice, does water
Choose to fall, and in the instant of that
Lovely decision lose all pity—like Homer's crow
Or the Spartan fox cub—becoming
Incorruptible, a zealot?

Mutual distinction, shared
Isolation, autobiography
Reflects in vain upon former comforts
Lost irrevocably now. Vermont

Is antiquity. The wood smoke
Curls in early morning constellation.

The cows are taller than school bells. Two children,
In different decades, guided me
To the same waterfall. I never could
Have found it on my own. I cannot find it now.
The past is stronger than life, choosing
To fall without help into fleshly diamond.

My own flesh is given to map-making, accumulating
Shapes in hapless preparation for nothing
Ever to happen…think of Auden's later face. I was
Below the walls of Troy at the bus stop. I gathered
Europa into my arms beneath the Christmas tree.
Places, and the names of places, are thus half fantasy.

Between pathos and love there is also
A cliff face for me, dry as dust, facing
The Missouri River. We climbed, finding
Our footholds in the rock, in the gaps
Between angels who allowed for us.
Reaching the top, we saw the river rise to us.

Angel, make nonsense of geography.
Likewise, the topographical chaos
Of faces, hair, the foreshortened places
Behind our knees, confound the angels.
How are they to find us in all the woodlands
And dust? Mistaking Missouri for Vermont,
Each is beyond hope, outraged

At the apex of deadfall. All depends
Upon outwardness, but no one told the boy.
Pity blinds a songbird, and no one tells the boy.
The small, impossibly white hand that led him
Up the cliff face dissolved into light

Glinting off the river there below.
The angel afterwards was a poor sort.
I want only that hand again: eider,
Antiquity. No whiteness ever since
Has equaled the whiteness of it,
That soft dream. All waters are the ghost of it.

Lost irrevocably now, imago
Fades into pathos and then into
The parting gesture of the form of forms.
The future wears a mist upon its finger.
It has a kiss in mind, and a shipwreck also—
One of those tall stories only the good know.

HATE SPEECH

For Claudia Keelan

We could live on the moon
By calendars of one color:
Days invisible but numberless,
Given to mass and to a perjured year.
Today is a day of jubilee.
Tomorrow will be the same,
Appareled in fires as fast as fires,
Burned to one color. Day by day,
A children's crusade clamors
Inside us. You were there with me.
People in cars shouted hateful words,
And then came bullets we could not see,
Could not count. Time might be
Anything, but strangely is a ghost of colors.

IN MEMORY OF DENISE LEVERTOV

A calm mind neither apparels
Nor judges the rained-upon zoo animals.
Anger only, as a child frustrated
With lions sleeping through midday,
Dresses them with terrors intact,
Damning them. Humanity is no bargain.
We've run out of options.

Kindness merely drags it out longer,
Letting the lions starve, too weak
Anymore to lift their mouths to the rain.
And of the angry martyr in me, less said
The better. There's terror in the milk.
Cruelly deprived of the civil cruelties,
We are beasts that never were, and lions die.

A HINT TO LUCRETIUS

The afterlife is an austere beast,
Fabulous but austere:
The most desired is charioteer
To the broken alto of the least,

Hobbled by aftermath but still
Beautiful, still with one bauble
Of scar upon her lip. Trouble
My mouth with your mouth. Fill

The rampant measures as Campion did.
Tabard is hue, and thyme is terrace.
My mother's name was Doris,
A Greek unknown to her. Hidden

Among the wild herbs in their patterns
Are first things, and first things never die.
To them, the afterlife is a memory.
When I was born, there were lanterns

Strung upon eyebeams to the horizon.
Nothing afterwards stretched so far.
Upon the early mind, there are
Two loves, each a white campion.

II

EASTER 2018

Was it noble,
The bitter austerity of desire

Opposing
Viol to cello, rampant to redoubled

Free animals,
Phaedrus a litter of souls coupled

Eternally?
There was a hillside farm, a steep one. I saw it.

It was slow to
Perish, floating in a mist of white bees.

Then later,
My face became strange to me.

The world also.
Charioteer of wounds and bleeding,

What herbs might help
My dead beneath the bright wheels of thousands

Of you? Wild thyme
Was a man once. The upshot and noon inclined

To apogee,
The higher still as early Magdalene.

THE SILVER HYPHENS

To my amazement, someone is dancing.
Eternal Biedermeier, the sound of windshield wipers
Lulling the car, making of the rain
A beloved shape-shift deeply, my sister's
Charm bracelet on the wheel rhyming "Ramapo"

With "Brahms' Alto," the sound is stronger than hills
Yielding to facts. This is my poem,
A paean to dementia. This embraces
Dementia. The rain conceals a little,
Then is wiped away. The next exit

Toys with the undercarriage gently.
Rain makes a gorgeous pattern on the glass.
Let us begin: we are driving in the rain.
Rampant, redoubled, sister and I see
The rain so beautiful and then an empty

Windshield equally deathless, dazzling
Winter bees with a mountain on each wing.
By noon, nothing remains but romantic litter.
Biedermeier at all the outposts beats,
Whirrs, thuds. One charm upon the bracelet

Rings my eye with emerald around.
The first word of the risen Christ was "Woman."
Did Magdalene require a further word?
Is there a forgotten country, *un pays vague*,
Behind the vexed and uxorious country

Forgotten just now? Litter of rain,
Little winter birds suggest as much. The aftermath
Of Bellerophon was olive groves. But see:
The shadows of olive trees turn instantly
To water. Waves of light, in a concourse

Of silver hyphens, drench new patterns of herbs
Near to home. Home is a southern studio.
Mother dotes upon a downing moon.
My sister drives a Biedermeier toy.
To my amazement, someone is dancing.

"THE SENSATION OF DEATH..."

The sensation of death—crepe and passageway,
Items and banners motionless despite the wind—
Is very much like driving. Clever Emily!

Flesh and wheel, flesh and wheel, bright
Particles spark at the edge of eyesight.
One older than myself veers off and is gone.

I am alone to imagine animals
Left and right, and a strength of animals
Along my spine, leaning in to death.

Eternity is fun, but there's no
Stopping it. Light batters light, the stars go
Haywire out of pattern, and my eyes

Are broken mirrors without me.

AMERICAN SUNLIGHT

> *Half our standards come from our first masters,*
> *and the other half from our first loves.* —George Santayana

Young people together—there never was
An image more pressing. In the ebon lapse
Of time, our slow damnation to continuities,
A pigeon loves hopelessly the cold, clay owl
Meant only to frighten her. Likewise,
Young people pause in a doorway fifty
And more years ago. I am one of them.
I am also here to one side, desperate
To image their youth-time to myself
Just once: clay to clay; owl to stone-cold owl.
One of them smiles to herself beneath her hair.
The doorway seems to part two fires.
Another slips her hand into a boy's back pocket,
Featherlight, and all of them laugh together.
The fires join. The doorway disappears.
For yet his noule was totty of the must,
And truly our youth-time was autumn
In the world—golden without and fire
Within. Just look at the hair. Just see
What human eyes see pressing upon a smile.
Today, memory and expectation
Join in a rhythm, and I know again
Perfectly each note of the *Requiem*
(KV 626). A hand in my back pocket

Conducts a doorway into the downing moon.

The sky echoes a swarm and an outcry.
Youth likewise frightens the world away
As hungry owls hunt autumn into a girl.
Featherlight October catches fire in her.
Upon her lips, the blissful curve of Spenser's
Strange theogony explains a dying man
To clouds of *tendresse*, a kind
Of dilation the oceans batter to accomplish
But cannot, overpowered by outcry.
I remember each note of it. It is only
The lull in the rhythm I lack, and breath.
Once again a Sheol of continuities
Mocks upon my eye. There is a photograph
Any one of a dozen boys might have taken,
Phaedrus of a kind though I cannot see
Any one of them, and so what use
Have I for eyes? Perpetual light
Is not Heaven if I cannot see
Their faces younger by half a moment
In the cold iris warming to them,
A flower they would later tend without me,
Opened wide, almost like collapsing.
Human eyes collapse, and that's as cold
A definition of memory as I can give.
Ruit arduus aether, and then I made
A rural pen and stained the water clear.
Did I imagine, as a way of meaning,
To separate creation from disaster?
I remember only the youth of things:

The first rain, latent until the railings gleamed;
Doors wide open and then filled with owls;
Pocket in hand, hand in pocket;
The struggling rose beneath a Joshua tree.
Si fractus illabatur orbis,
Impavidum ferient ruinae,
As Horace says, meaning that the very
Soul of ruin collapses into one word
After another, creating new souls,
Rushing to disaster as to the youth of things.
For so long, Eden served as a byword
For sunlight, the curve of a strand of hair
Blown upon a smile, a wrist, a feather
Refusing to fall. Young people together
By no accident lean into loves.
With no sound, Heaven ruins from Heaven.
Eden hunts into a girl and is forgotten
Like the shadow of a hand just before
A rough hand captures it and it is gone.

One upon another, the ancients lean towards love.
The light overtops itself in smallest leaves,
Itself the least of all these pressing upon
Glass. If I were to press my hand
Onto the topmost window, it would leave
The imprint of a flare or of two branches
Extended: boy and girl; apple and apple;
Archaic impulse to forget and archaic
Remembrance. The window bursts into one
Thousand elements of rain. Water
Is the leaf of light, and merely to lay hands

Onto the gleam of it overtops the trees.
Whenever I met your eyes in the morning,
Such antiquity as never faded
Out of the world gleamed into elements
Of upreach, apples, and the love of God.
Sweet memory and endless hassle
Gleamed Alpha, gleamed the wet of the new world.

American sunlight is a different
Measure in both the strings and the woodwinds,
Different bright stones under flowing water.
What is constant in the bones of horse and wheel
Riots near to Hudson and Housatonic.
Yes, Jesus loves me. A dragonfly
Came a very long way over water,
Touching one stone after another,
Just to tell me so. Gather a river
From the broken window of me. Open it
Crazy onto the rain, and surely you will know
A perishing weather has opened to you.
O, she is the elder May, a Mary.
Things of August auroral set her feet
Dancing upon gleams and dragonflies
When there will be no winters anymore.
Mr. Arcady Ives has a surprise in store:
Top and bottom of wings; the shining shore.

No civic ardor prevents or bends,
Nor organ voluntary instantly
Tyrannical ever quite equals
The austerity and unquiet topsy-
Turvy havering in the organ loft
Of Mr. Ives. My wife and I stopped
At the side of the road to listen.
The hand of God rested. Hudson
And Housatonic flowed backwards a moment,
Just a moment long enough. *Si fractus*
Illabatur orbis, impavidum
Ferient ruinae. Heaven ruining
From Heaven parted the trees,
And three boys stepped forth into the sunshine.
Hercules, Pollux, and one other
Who had burned to death stepped out into the light.
The river flowed on. My wife and I drove on.

My wife, my color, my car and my
Ruining sense of time begin to blend
Into a weather of bees whitening
Hillsides with their final noise. I would have liked
To write something like the *Georgics*, but
I haven't the art or earth. All the ground
I own slopes away out of memory
Full speed, black as a wrist dearly
Braceleted with shadows clashing and clanging
Dark music. Something has slammed a door shut.
Something means to keep us in the car.
Ruit arduus aether...before and after
Stand giants of sunlight, archaic and clear.

As music becomes more familiar,
It hurries, repeating the phrase of hillsides
In higher registers and then higher.
Patches of snow seem to be walking
Swathed in rain, then in grass, and then in
Strange lights wearing the treble white of boys.
Destroy all the monuments you can find,
There is still a revival marching brass
From steeple to steeple. There is still
An affirmation lording the sun
With youth, with daring, with a weird halloo.
If ever I remember anything
Just as it was, a crazy boy will lead me.
His mania is every hillside I can name.

This is a poem about dementia
Wandering a nation without memory,
America devoted now to abandoning
Its monuments and its younger me
Wasp-waisted into delves of oblivion.
May you never see your son in shackles.
May his image raise battalions from the earth.
May patches of cloud swathing a peach orchard
Walk to meet him at the crest of his ferocity.
May the wars of kindness find him steadfast and free.

The doubtless piety of bird and branch,
One a continuing miracle to the other
Weighting certainty with nothing but air,
Marks the inhuman world with a flourish.
What about me? In my first youth, I read

Signs in everything, and in good time
I could alternate feather with feather,
Star with meteor and, sometimes, yellow hair.
Collapsed into his effort, a hawk
Ruins out of the punishing August air
Onto no prey. He is the sign of youth
Outdated and alone. Now that I am old,
The greased wick of a helmeted airman,
I am a token to others unlike me.
I am one truce and one message.
I am the sharpest word a hillside ever
Spoke. Trim, trim the rain as it fell the first time
You can remember. It was a wick afire
Gathering blackness into itself,
Driving it deep into the earth and into
The memory of new life, green without rain.
If we are not compelled, we are fortunate
Freely to abandon memory.
The young will not feel the burden of it.
The hills will seem taller to them, and shadows
Softer than I could ever recall
Safely move and safely graze on surface lights.
My lecture notes are running away from me.
There was something very important
About Dante and a dream surfacing
In Ravenna. It doesn't matter now.
What eludes me has dearly become myself

As I appear to others unknown to me.
I am a faint light doused in the clamor
Of their strange eyes freshening
Vision's boyhood and the good courage
Of one girl bold enough to look away.

SAVED FOR LATER

*I had never heard Rameau on the ukulele,
but the effect was both modest and graceful.* —John Glassco

We live in a time of relentless
Sensual negations, a barrel of monkeys
Overfilled with corrections inspired by
Utopian hacks misreading Baudelaire
Or by menace of blackface mocking
The old gods with gods even older, even
More gaily inclined to easeful despair.
When I allude, let it stick to you.
Unhorsed, reinvent the animal,
And it will find you deep in the dark wood.
Reinvent the wheel, and it will speed you
Deep into the wild pig's wounded Adonis.
You see what I mean about old gods.
Covet other angels, *Anno Domini*.

To hills still green with early love and herbs
Medicinal, the quiet of deep concern
Falls at a steep angle, *frei aber einsam*,
Sparkling like a snow of trouble untroubled
Suddenly by one horse willing to stand still.
Faith and heroism, *tendresse* in that singular
Perfection that puts an end to thought
Precisely where no further thought is required,
Pattern the calendars of a child on tiptoe.

Early love changes with the seasons,
Remaining early love. My words allude
To mothering and to the hues of snow
Just at sunrise. God is just. And because
Of light hands in the alto, His law is love.

Are my unremembered ones deprived of me
Or I of them? As law is the love driving
Memory to distraction, would it not be
Just as easy to turn my eyes away,
Forgetting the roads ahead and those behind me,
Entrusting myself to those rainy hillsides
Shaping heroism, faith, and *tendresse*
Tall alongside? I'm so happy to see them!
Names and faces, faces and names, these
Are distractions. Memory distrusts me.
Nevertheless I am happy to entrust
Myself to blinding rain, just as the young Christ
Was happy to give his entire weight
To a single blade of grass, oh strange bee!

I have but mistaken futility
All this while, just as celestials, driving
Into the white woods of life everlasting
Mistake their helplessness for peril and cry
Out. Whiteness is the light by which to read
Blinding rain in blackface by a downing moon.
Stop crying. The planet is ready to die.
It was a bubble, and cursive panes of color
Shatter inwardly in the Latin: *Bulla,
Bulla*. The arc of the ache of it

Alludes to misshapen pains now put right.
The farms are standing taller than the hills.
They are heaven at hand and no memory.
Covet no more martyrs, *Anno Domini*.

A DOE ON A PEACH

For Pam Rehm

Nearly impossible sweetness, and color
Beyond labor gather the woods into one
Thought, one sensation. The place of miracle
Is to be out of place the one time
Reality wants repair. At the edge
Of the woods, a woman is dying.
Her husband's gone mad with grief,
Disappearing into the effort of grief,
Leaving her the free space of a window
On amplitude as far as the tree line.
A thrown peach troubles the grass with sunshine.
A glistening upon a shadow parts the trees.
Unamazed, in only delight, the doe eats
Until the grass is once again itself.

WHITE CAMPION

> *If we meet each other in Hell it's not Hell.*
> —Geoffrey Hill

The angel of thrill begins
In a lost room darkly paneled,
Gaping to the open air like wild
Flowers, like arrows,
To sing the human mind.

He is no effigy.
He attends to miracles
As you and I attend to
Open wounds, birth pangs
Actually like wild flowers

Fletched, forgiving, free
As the campion moth to be itself
And two into a later bargain:
All that is made.

1.

How is it I can never find
Or call to mind
One image of Christ walking slowly in the rain,
In a steady, gentle rain,
The kind that shapes an afterimage

Just for a moment of the man
Like a cloak of shadow following
Or like a blank page
After it's been turned?
The dead are concealed from us
But not distorted by the rain.
They remember our having remembered.
A woman curls up on the sofa.
Years before the fact, she sleeps
Her death and drapes it
Even now, exactly as she must.

Just after dawn,
In the wren's eye
There are no blossoms left in the trees
And yet the sunlight blazons white
New flowers onto every leaf.
The wren's eye gorges itself,
Bursting the new life.
The memory of a tree is the tree.
Christ could fly.
Impale upon him certain words
Good as Greek
For the impulse of the earth is to seek
A language of flowers
That do not die, turning
A hair's breadth towards us
Even now, exactly as they must.

If it was justice I saw
Fall from the sun
Onto boys ruining the one
Flower shared between them,
So be it.
The woman on the sofa wears a little wing
In her sleep. When she awakes,
Its twin will be the wren in the dream
Nearly there, nearly all the way
There, nearly all the way
There into the human day.
Rain falls out of brilliant sunshine.
For a moment, her window
Fills with catastrophe, boys
Torn apart and scattered, white petals
Blackening the glass,
Exacting recent justice.

So strange that the recent past,
As chaste
As antiquity, as the orangery
Of a blind eye, should at once appear
Preposterous
Yet achingly tender.
Modern times are too cautious.
The boyish, florid love of catastrophe
Has thrust a fist into the dawn,
And the scent of that fist,
Whose citron betters daylight,
Is wasted on modern times.
Not long ago, you and I

Nearly captured a wren.
Christ lifted his face then,
And rain fell all day until evening.

2.

In a corner of my garden, there is a spider's web
Entirely armored in rose petals broken off by rain.
The spider will learn to eat roses, or he will starve to death.
This is political economy for modern times.
The planet dies. The planet starves its cruel interiors
First, with a blazon of colors and soft poetry. Next,
It apportions one small bird to every tree and sets fire
To the tree. The rest is the cold business of the oceans
Who have never forgiven us for breathing air.
Homer was tempted. Loose thighs of oblivion
Welcomed humanity away from itself and from life,
And only one out of the Bronze-Age host refused that welcome.
He was the father of starvation, entirely armored
In the disguise of a real man, destroyer of oceans.
We have made an ugly war upon distinctions.
Canon bleeds a wedding into the gigue, and "when
I try to imagine a faultless love or" the seedtime
Of my deepest convictions—that the soul is immortal,
That a woman couched upon a fragile, little wing
Created the creator of the universe—thought,
Or rather the entire machinery of truth and terror
Usurps a newborn king, i.e. imagination.
Phaedrus, step down. There is a little wing wearing sunshine
Like wind in the white hair of the bee you never imagined.
An infinitesimal distance goes on forever.

At the moment of death, the light hand of Attic stele
Softly lights upon the shoulder of eternity,
And thought yields to flesh and flesh yields to imagination,

Sexing this or that unimaginable creation
With new hair. It makes a difference. We are bound to one another
And to God by harrowing, albeit helpless distinctions,
Impossible to bridge, imperative to love well.
We are free, but briefly. The pattern of a leaf branches
Out from human hearts, and the blood spills
Into the pattern a stone makes crashing into windshields.
God follows. The wrist and wing of the Beloved follow
Close behind, and not even Hell prevails against
This new extinction. Slow time is the beginning
Of no time at all. The light hand of Attic stele
Wrests me from the sleep I'd imagined life to be,
The walking stone, the irreparable Gesthemane,
And I am awake, wearing the green flesh newly-fashioned
From my heart.

CODA

Should the bird outlast the last blossom in the tree?
Keep faith, but keep it silently,
Starveling.

I keenly remember there were two of us,
And a stand of poplars like a kiss
Quavering

Upon the shade of the earth where no earth was

Ready to bear the weight of us
Relinquishing

Soul for substance, pistil of white campion
For color, continuance and one
Unbelieving

Substance of perfect memory.
There were no trees.
The sun was shining.

WHEN I DIE

> *We shelter an angel whom we never cease to offend.*
> *We ought to be the guardians of that angel.* —Jean Cocteau

A scherzo of thumbnail butterflies, white ones,
Covers the hillside. God is more
Adorable than music. Nevertheless,
On a given morning, as the wind drops,
Music pries Heaven apart from itself,
Like flowers beneath the wings unfolded on them.

Every breeze is self-registering.
This morning, I walked deeper into the hill,
Free of the sun. Midway up the tallest trees,
One leaf alone would stir while all the leaves
On the very same branch remained stock-still.
Apart from itself, Heaven signaled to me.

William Blake was no romantic. He was,
Beyond the arsons of levity and his toe,
The final bulwark of the baroque.
He was the last to oppose, "almost
Successfully," rebirth on all the wrong terms.
He saw the leaf alone where no light was.

Infinite variation plays against
A steadfast variety. The butterfly
Knows the difference in its wings, even

As the flower she alights upon darkens
Beneath her weight. The sun goes deeper
Into the hill. Root systems riot and shine.

Did you think for a moment Earth
Was aware of itself? Never. Its adoration
Persists altogether elsewhere from
The very beginning, beginning again
Just at that moment one leaf all alone
Spins into the baroque, a scherzo of one note.

The hillside is covered with little doors,
And the wind rises out of them, returning,
When the music is spent, with all the news
Of the unaware, unreflecting, nearly perfect
Hours blindly about the business of perfection.
Hence the tiny eyes on a butterfly's wing.

Rebirth is an idiot. Isolated
Each into its own eternity,
Like every pain, birth continues out of mind
Deeper into the hill. Earth riots
With levity. Darkness swims into light.
Flowers begin to imagine the life of flowers.
Heaven signals to me, pouring down shade
Out of the canopy of trees, prying

The sunlight apart from itself. Darkness
And light are the same thing. Music moves
Effortlessly between the two, made of nothing
But wings, wings with eyes, no end in sight.

THE MEASURE

It is child's play, creatures too perfectly
Disguised for the hawk's notice, even
As the hawk screams. Retreating shadows,
Mother and child play at immortality.

Age it forward. The hawk consents. Although
He may well starve, he consents, dropping
One feather in praise of the resistless
Intelligence of the moment and its realism.

Our shadows are eternity's accurate
Measurement of time; they retreat, and so
Eternity takes shelter among
The creatures, *as* a creature: Christmas

On a given Wednesday, housed by feathers.
What hope is the hawk? We live forever
In the cool shade of his pain and noise.
We are disguised by what he cannot eat.

Beautiful measures denude his tree,
And even he, perhaps he most of all,
Screams delight into catastrophe.
Destitution is a small price to pay

For life everlasting in the sketch of light
Outlining shadows. And by that I mean nothing
More than the whisper of evidence: death.
I mean the disguise of your mother and of mine.

We were small, and we were taken to safety.
A barbed arrow of sound pierced the air
Overhead, making a pause in creation.
That was the beginning of beauty.

NOTES

"*Senesco sed amo*": "I age, but I love."

Menippus (3rd century BC): The Cynic satirist from whom Menippean Satire takes its name.

Lucian (120 AD-192 AD): A Syrian satirist.

"*Ingenium nobis ipsa puella fecit*": "My genius is no more than a girl."—Sextus Propertius (50 BC-15 BC).

"*Deus nec laedit amantes*": "God does not harm lovers."—Albius Tibullus (died 19 BC).

"*Ubi amor, ibi oculus est*": "Where there is love, there is the eye."—Richard of St. Victor, Scottish philosopher and mystical theologian (1110-1173).

"*Omnia quae sunt, lumina sunt*": "All things that are are lights."—Johannes Scotus Erigena, Irish theologian and poet (815-877).

Frei aber einsam: "Free but lonely"—motto of violinist Joseph Joachim, close friend and collaborator of Johannes Brahms. Brahms used the motto (F-A-E) as a motif for his first symphony.

Recent Titles from Alice James Books

Last Days, Tamiko Beyer
If This Is the Age We End Discovery, Rosebud Ben-Oni
Pretty Tripwire, Alessandra Lynch
Inheritance, Taylor Johnson
The Voice of Sheila Chandra, Kazim Ali
Arrow, Sumita Chakraborty
Country, Living, Ira Sadoff
Hot with the Bad Things, Lucia LoTempio
Witch, Philip Matthews
Neck of the Woods, Amy Woolard
Little Envelope of Earth Conditions, Cori A. Winrock
Aviva-No, Shimon Adaf, Translated by Yael Segalovitz
Half/Life: New & Selected Poems, Jeffrey Thomson
Odes to Lithium, Shira Erlichman
Here All Night, Jill McDonough
To the Wren: Collected & New Poems, Jane Mead
Angel Bones, Ilyse Kusnetz
Monsters I Have Been, Kenji C. Liu
Soft Science, Franny Choi
Bicycle in a Ransacked City: An Elegy, Andrés Cerpa
Anaphora, Kevin Goodan
Ghost, like a Place, Iain Haley Pollock
Isako Isako, Mia Ayumi Malhotra
Of Marriage, Nicole Cooley
The English Boat, Donald Revell
We, the Almighty Fires, Anna Rose Welch
DiVida, Monica A. Hand
pray me stay eager, Ellen Doré Watson

Alice James Books is committed to publishing books that matter. The press was founded in 1973 in Boston, Massachusetts as a cooperative, wherein authors performed the day-to-day undertakings of the press. This element remains present today, as authors who publish with the press are invited to collaborate closely in the publication process of their work. AJB remains committed to its founders' original feminist mission, while expanding upon the scope to include all voices and poets who might otherwise go unheard. In keeping with its efforts to build equity and increase inclusivity in publishing and the literary arts, AJB seeks out poets whose writing possesses the range, depth, and ability to cultivate empathy in our world and to dynamically push against silence. The press was named for Alice James, sister to William and Henry, whose extraordinary gift for writing went unrecognized during her lifetime.

Designed by
PAMELA A. CONSOLAZIO

Spark design

PRINTED BY MCNAUGHTON & GUNN